HISTORICAL CATS

First published in Great Britain in 2003

10 9 8 7 6 5 4 3 2 1

British Library Cataloguing in Publication Data
A record for this book is available from the British Library

ISBN 0 340 86221 1

Design by Janette Revill

Printed and bound in Italy by Printer Trento

Hodder & Stoughton
A Division of Hodder Headline Ltd
338 Euston Road
London NW1 3BH
www.madaboutbooks.com

HISTORICAL CATS

GREAT CATS WHO HAVE SHAPED HISTORY

Heather Hacking

Hodder & Stoughton

LONDON SYDNEY AUCKLAND

KING TUTANKHAMIN 'n' KHAMOUT

THIS YOUNG KING of Ancient Egypt was the 'golden boy' of 1350 BC. Not only was he a god-king, he was also a brilliant inventor. His most famous and useful invention was a catflap for pyramids. Until then, his ancestors, the undead Kings of the Nile, had to keep getting up from their immortal slumber to let the cat out, and what with wandering about secret corridors and bumping into scary statues in the dark, some of the late-departed monarchs were becoming very short of sleep and rather on edge. The resourceful Tut is depicted here with his devoted young wife, Mrs Tut. She is offering a model of his amazing triangular catflap and he is holding another of his inspirations: the two-speed fly-whisk.

MEWSES

*W*HETHER IT WAS the pressure of wearing a silly wig in searing heat or the ever-present agitation about dying before the completion of the interior decoration of one's tomb, we will never know, but life was one long fret for phuraohs. To relieve the tension they often took it out on the slaves, so it was no surprise to anyone when one long, hot summer in the Nile Valley, the phuraoh petulantly decided all slave tom-kittens would be rounded up and wiped out. Mewses' mother hid her son in a cat basket and floated it down the Nile. He was found in the bullrushes by the phuraoh's daughter and was taken to the palace and raised as a pet. From here, he was able to see the inside workings of the king's mind and it was not a pretty sight.

Mewses decided it was time to move the slaves out of Egypt. He asked God for instructions.

'Easy,' replied God. 'I'll distract the Egyptians with a plague of frogs while you round up the lads and get them out into the desert.' As there are few things more distracting

God and Mewses fixing the phuraoh with frogs

than frogs dropping from the sky, Mewses was easily able to lead the slaves into the desert. Then God opened up a path across the Red Sea. 'Off you go to the land of milk and munchies, and … you look a bit peaky … come and see me about taking some tablets.'

MIAOWPATRA

THIS BEAUTIFUL, EXTRAVAGANT, tortoiseshell Queen of the Nile, seen trying to get a bite on her barque, was descended from the famous Phuraohs of Ancient Egypt. She was of the age of Ptolemy: a time when Egyptian

Miaowpatra is gently lowered into her bath

rulers were peace-loving, educated and ptolerant. It was also an age of travel, reason and romance, and this queen is well remembered as the beloved of two glorious Roman leaders: Julius (Jellymeat) Caesar and his former ally, Whiskas Antonius. It was hard for her to choose between these two noble Romans but she finally settled for the latter (9 out of 10 Egyptian queens who expressed a preference preferred Whiskas).

She died tragically young after an unfortunate error at a regal banquet when, instead of eating a jellied eel, she mistakenly picked up an un-jellied asp.

Miaowpatra gives Caesar the heave-ho

ALICKSANDER THE GREAT

*T*HIS YOUNG HEART-THROB was known as 'Alicksander the Great Left Foot' or 'the Paw of God'. He took his soccer team, Macedonia United, to victory after victory in which the Greeks were gutted, the Persians were pulverised and the Nubians nobbled. After he had forced Darius of the Persian Blues into early retirement in the Then Known World Cup, it looked as though 'Licksy' had no great competition left. So he married the fluffy Roxanne and spent most of his time being well-groomed and looking moody in sunglasses, sometimes in the Greek national costume, the short, white skirt. Wax tabloids of the day had something to say about this.

CLAWDIUS

*C*LAWDIUS WAS THE unlikely successor to the throne of ancient Rome. Clawdius was the first in his family, and a long line of empurrors, to show a streak of sanity. This was despite his pronounced limp (an old mouse-trap wound) and an afflicting stammer that made his purr-purring sound like an ancient Fiat Uno idling at the traffic lights – he could not have been more unlike his megalomaniac relatives.

His crazy cousin, the then Empurror Catigula, had been accidentally deified one afternoon at the temple of Pusseidon. Catigula had yowled: 'I would like a bit of

Catigula is gathered to the gods

*The lives of empurrors were quite short
and dangerous*

cod', but, owing to low-lying cloud around Mount
Olympuss, it had been received as 'I would like to be a god!'
– and in a flash of lightning, the mad ruler was gathered into
the bosom of his ancestors. This left Clawdius the only one
left to run the empurror business as the Royal Palace had
been severely depopulated by the family mania for sharpening their claws on close relatives. When all the fur had settled there was standing-room only at the royal mausoleum.

BODICE-EAR

ＴHIS NOBLE AND ferocious queen has been described by Roman chroniclers as having red, flowing fur and a voice so harsh that it could crack open an oyster at ten paces.

She had two great preoccupations in life – spending money and removing Romans. The latter had recently

A Roman informer helping Bodice-Ear with her enquiries

marched into Britain uninvited and, with a good deal of clatter, constructed a Roman capital city slap opposite Bodiceear's palace at Colchester. The Queen's topaz eyes glittered with annoyance as she quietly basted a roasting Roman informer. She vowed to reduce the Roman city to ashes. However, she had a difficult dilemma: the capital contained a brand-new shopping mall packed with interesting shops. She resolved this conundrum by belting up and down the aisles of Colchester Safeway in her 1.5 GTi chariot relieving the store of its best canned salmon. *Then* she set fire to the city. It may be argued that she cooked her goose by this action, since nothing annoys an expatriate Roman more than the fragrance of crispy, fried forum and a foreign, pyromaniac woman driver.

Bodice-Ear negotiates Roman traffic police

ERIK THE VIKING

CALLED 'RATSCOURGE' AND 'Mousedeath', this fearless Viking roved the North Sea and plundered the Saxon shores in pursuit of loot, pillage and new, improved, rabbit-recipe 'Whiskas'.

Terrible sagas were told, embroidered by legend, of the Vikings' plundering of the Northern mousteries. The entire holy order of St Eek!lesiastes, on the island of Iona, was put to flight in a single night of flying fur.

Erik's reign of terror was ended when he was finally felled by the iron claw of the English warlord, Anlaf Eathelferret. The spirit of the Viking hero was carried across the water on his funeral longship, to the herring grounds of the Skaggarak and onward to the great hall of the Norse god, Odin.

An ancestor of the Normans, Erik's lusty blood pulsated in the veins of many warlords including Duke William the Canker-ear of Normandy. In 1066, William invaded England and overthrew the Anglo-Saxon monarchy. This marked the beginning of French being taught in secondary schools throughout England: thus did proud Erik have his revenge upon the House of Eathelferret.

Ethel and Erik the Viking at Safeway, Malmo

RICHARD THE FURRED

THIS KING HAS been much maligned by history. It was put about for centuries that he had murdered the young pilchards in the Tower. However, this now seems unlikely as early records show that some of Richard's best friends had fins. Nor was Richard a deformed hunchback – he just wasn't very good at putting on his tights.

Richard has trouble with his tights

*Caterwauling contest
at Bosworth*

The real villain was probably that arch-propagandist, Henry VII, the first Chewed-Ear king. He eventually beat Richard in a caterwauling contest at a packed Bosworth stadium. Henry could wail louder and longer than Richard, so the King conceded defeat with his famous whisper:

'I'm hoarse, I'm hoarse – my kingdom for a ...'

Thus the last of the Plantagenets was silenced.

GENGHIS KHAT

A FEARLESS HORSEMAN, seen here with his fiery steed, Merrylegs, Genghis swept across the great plains and up and down the windswept steppes in search of more competitive gymkhanas, ruthlessly snapping up all the red rosettes and silver cups. Having plundered everything in sight, he dieted furiously and became a world-famous jockey. He snaffled the Samarkand Trophy (304 miles over the jumps), bagged the Cheltenham Gold Cup and was the first foreign feline to win the Kentucky Derby. He then retired and founded a dynasty of top jockeys. These included the fabled Kublai Khat, a course and distance winner at Xanadu, who, in celebration of his illustrious grandfather, a stately pleasure dome decreed.

CHRISTOFUR COLUMPUSS

Ｋ ING FURRED-HAND AND Queen Isabella of Spain wanted to find the short unscenic route to the precious Spice Islands of the Orient; it was then the vogue to have your sardines very peppered. They really could not have picked a worse navigator for the job than C. Columpuss.

All should have been plain sailing, but Columpuss turned right instead of left at Gibraltar. After weeks at sea, all the fleet had sighted was neat, undiluted brine and rations were already beginning to run short. Even the rats abandoned ship in disgust and the situation looked black when a weary albatross refused to land on deck. The men commented bitterly that the only terra firma they had seen so far was that situated under the captain's hat.

As the weary, wet episode wore on, the crew became mutinous and Columpuss often had to take refuge in the crow's nest, much to the consternation of the crow. Just as the sailors were preparing a lynch party with Christofur as the guest of honour, the captain and the crow cried 'Land

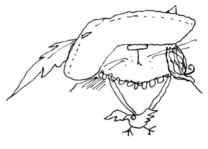

Columpuss models his 'albatross necklace'
– a present from the crew

Ahoy!' as the fleet collided gently with the coast of San Salvador.

Ignoring the fact that the U.S. customs officials were busily throwing the cargo of teabags overboard, that his crew had raced down to a hamburger bar and that there was a fresh Cherokee arrow ornamenting his left ear, Columpuss insisted that he had arrived in the East Indies. He remained adamantly convinced of this as he lived out the rest of his days in the New World, sporadically sending back postcards to Spain remarking thereon how much the style of the national costume had changed since Marco Polo's days.

MONTEZUMA
THE AZ-TICK CHIEF

MONTEZUMA WAS THE proud, noble leader of the Az-tick civilisation in Central America. They survived by scratching a living; they had loads of chocolate but no tick-powder. Their plumed serpent-god, Quetzalcoatl, sailed eastwards, promising to return with a hope of a solution. Eventually some speck of hope was bound to reappear on the radiant blue Atlantic waters. Unfortunately and misleadingly, the speck in question was the marauding chocolate mouse-hunter, the Spaniard Furnando Clawtez, sporting plumed armour and hissing with his normal ill-humour.

The furry, feather-coated, cat serpent-god suffering an identity crisis

The confused natives gave Clawtez the freedom of the city and acquainted the Spanish with the delights of chocolate mice *and* creamy hot chocolate. Clawtez kindly responded by introducing the Az-ticks to ancient Spanish customs like theft and mayhem. Before conceding his kingdom and chocolate mines to the conquistadores, Montezuma invoked the traditional curse of 'Pepacatahotbotl', which roughly translates as 'being bitten on the backside by a plumed serpent', and any European traveller to Mexico who has tasted jalapeño peppers will know what this means.

Az-tick chocolate mouse production line

THE PAWGIA FAMILY

RENAISSANCE ITALY IN the sixteenth century was overshadowed and terrified by the powerful House of Pawgia. Alicksander Pawgia bribed and wheedled his way into becoming Pope in times when a Pope could have anything he could get his greedy, acquisitive claws on. But he was positively frugal compared to his wicked son, Cesare, pictured here with his sister, Lucretia. Cesare didn't care much for cats that weren't family, so sprinkled rat-poison on their spaghetti (*Warfarin Parmegianno*). Lucretia soon took up the family apothecary-and-despatch business and her famous dish of *Calamari alla Strychinino* was reputed to have removed two husbands, one tax inspector, three traffic wardens and six passers-by.

After years of terror, the downfall of the House of Pawgia came when, at a banquet to celebrate the Pope's birthday, they let Lucretia do the cooking.

Bowled over by
Lucretia's calamari

SILLIMAN THE MAGNIFICAT

*H*ERE STANDS AN all-powerful despot who managed to take over half the known world without getting out of his pyjamas and shower cap. Silliman was the ruler of the Ottoman Empire (also the Richmond Odeon and the Ipswich Alhambra). In fact, as he swept across the map with

his mongrel hordes, he became the largest cinema chain owner from Samarkand to Vienna. On acquiring a new cinema, he ripped out all the existing seating – he was not the merciful sort. He then replaced the seats with silk ottomans, deeply upholstered, ideal for lounging on and sharpening claws.

Silliman selling tickets at the Ottoman Empire

*Silliman had his own way of dealing with
pigeons on his cinema roofs*

Today, it is still possible to see cinemas that reflect the
Silliman influence, with gold squiggles on the ceiling, etc.,
but the original ottomans have long since been replaced with
very hard seating equipped with a strong spring mechanism
that makes it double both as a seat and a mousetrap.

HENRY CHEWED-EAR

$\mathcal{T}$'HE LIFE AND reign of this magnificent monarch were dedicated to maintaining his fine bodyweight and appeasing his huge and fickle appetite; to which end he married six wives in search of a good cook.

Firstly, he married Cafurrine of Aragon in order to get his paws on the Spanish sardine rights; but soon he was sick of sild, so he divorced her in order to marry Spam Boleyn. He moved on to marry Anne-Chovy of Cleves, only to discover that Flemish cooking was so bad that her

A Tudor-court circle

'saddle of lamb' tasted mostly of saddle. He packed her off on a cookery course and married the delightful Jane Seyfood, a chip shop heiress from Devizes. She kept him happily supplied with cod and chips until she was tragically lost at sea when her trawler collided with the *Mary Rose*.

Then Henry married the young and pretty Kattyrine Howfurred. However, she was soon removed to the Tower when Henry discovered cookie crumbs in his courtiers' beds. In disillusioned old age, Henry settled down with his sixth and most caring wife, Kattyryn Purr, who administered his chicken soup with devotion.

Henry enjoys a cod and chip supper

William

Shakespaw!
Shakespurr!
Shakypooh

WILLIAM SHAKESPURR

*A*ROUND THE MIDDLE of the sixteenth century, entertainment in London had become somewhat sparse. There was the odd pageant or public hanging, but nothing really special. The only regular distraction was the Globe Theatre in Southwark. The theatre consisted of one round goldfish bowl haunted by two bored fish going round in pretty much the same old circles.

William Shakespurr, fresh from his success as entertainments manager at the Stratford Seaquarium, took over the Globe and installed a much larger aquarium complete with three plaster pyramids and a plastic palm tree, then re-introduced the two fish as *Anchovy and Cleopatra*. The crowd went wild. Encouraged, he started using shoals of thousands and stage-managed a wonderful *Herring the Fifth* with its rousing speech 'Once more unto the beach, dear friends ...' Soon he had written *A Midsummer Night's Bream* and *The Taming of the Shrew* (later renamed *Kiss Me Skate*), and *Trawlers and Cressida*.

QUEEN ELIZAPUSS I

$\mathcal{H}$ERE IS THE tetchy, flame-headed monarch known as 'Good Queen Puss' with her pomander, Ratty. She is rallying her navy of sea-cats: 'I may have the body of a cute and fluffy kitten,' she announced (she was a mistress of self-deception), 'but I have the heart and stomach of a bulldog.' Her beloved pirates raced off to get her a boatload of duty-frees. Sir Walthair Raleigh returned from America with the first potato crisps for his queen. 'Are they gin flavour?' she rasped. 'No, Ma'am' was the sort of reply that could get one into the Tower by sunset. Her distant cousin, the freckled cutie, Mewly, Queen of Spots, asked tweetily if she could take over running the country. That

The queen attends the Royal Première of Anchovy and Cleopatra *at the Globe Theatre*

44

set Elizapuss off on a hissing and spitting spat that could only be soothed by booty. 'Drake, duckie,' she purred at Sir Francis, 'Go an' attack somefink, somefink with jewels on it …' Drake and the boys shot off and the first bejewelled item they spotted was the Spanish entrant for the Cowes Week Yacht Races – the Armada. The English sailors grabbed pearl necklaces, Inca gold, gallons of best Rioja, the king's beard, bowls of tapas and a Julio Iglesias CD. Their queen was well happy. They celebrated with a lock-in at the Globe until 5 a.m.

ALL-OVER-FUR CROMWELL

CIVIL WARS CAN start over the smallest things. Cromwell liked highly polished armour, stiff, white collars, starched underpants and *detested* anything frilly or frivolous. The ruling monarch, King Charles, the Cavalier Spaniel, had long, curly ears and was up to his armpits in lace and high heels – so he had to go – and Cromwell became Lord Protector. He protected the cat population of England from bright colours, velvet cushions, ruffled curtains, catnip balls with bells on, toy goldfish on twangy elastic and anything

Cromwell checks that his warts aren't having too much fun

47

tasty or appealing. He was about as much fun as a wet night on a shed roof. His warts had more of a life than he did. The populace were bored rigid and the moment All-Over-Fur expired they replaced him with a new King Charles Spaniel and six months of feasting and tickling.

Puritan preachers

BLUEY THE XIV

*T*HIS EXQUISITE BLUE Persian ruled France, single-clawed, for most of the seventeenth century, maintaining his own personal luxury, fabulous arrogance and several rolls of fat. His glittering court at the Palace of Fursailles was devoted to indulgence, comfort and him. '*Après moi, tout est culottes* (after me, all is pants),' he declared.

He was, if anything, an overstated dresser, mostly seen mincing along in silk stockings, big knickers and his mother's beaded slingbacks, and real, live ermines slung nonchalantly over his arm. His life of *tulle* cushions, *noblesse* embraces and Normandy cream served him well – he outlived everybody else.

*Bluey minces
down to breakfast*

MOUSART

*P*RODIGIOUS, PRECOCIOUS, PRETTY – there are not enough 'P's to describe this mischievous young musician, who accidentally composed *Eine Kleine Nacht Mouse-eek!* (a small midnight snack) whilst chasing a prospective meal along the keyboard.

'Wolfie' was extremely fond of his food and passionately composed *You shall have a little fishy in a little dishy, Shrimp boats are a-coming*, and the very moving lovers' aria *Somewhere there's a plaice for us* which, in turn, inspired Schubert's *Trout* and caused Beethoven to regret the loss of his herring.

SAMUEL SQUEEKS THE DIARIST

*D*URING THE REIGN of the second King Charles Spaniel, Samuel obtained a high position in the Naval Offices. This was unfortunate as he hated water, so he turned to writing his *Diary of Dairy: A History of Cream*. He chronicled the Great Fire of London, which began in Pudding Lane where a chef was attempting to invent *crème brûlée*. Unfortunately he let the crème get over-brûlée-ed and small pan fire ensued. This spread to a wig factory, then to a false whisker emporium, on to a beauty spot manufacturers, then to Nell Gywn's frilly knicker factory, and suddenly, all of London was in flames. Poignantly, Samuel writes:
'We were reduced to

*Nell Gwyn demonstrates 'Dances with Oranges'
to Samuel Squeeks*

putting out the flames with flagons of best double Jersey!' A complete flirt, Sammy's ardour glowed as brightly as the embers of St Paul's cat hotel – occasionally milkmaids had to chuck a bucket of chilled semi-skimmed over him too.

NAPOLEON
FISHBONE-APART

'FISHBONE' WAS A fighter from the start. Tough and gritty, he always won, and he realised that with every victory, he gained territory. Perched on the Alps, catching up on a little claw polishing and feeling a niggling jot of tedium coming on, 'Fishbone' eyed France and thought 'Why not?' So, with the long-suffering chef and his pans clattering along

Street fighting in Ajaccio

in tow to celebrate each victory, creating a succession of *Scampi Provençales* and *Cod Lyonnaises*, Napoleon soon arrived in Paris, scratched but triumphant, and crowned himself Emperor of France and the Holy Roman Everything.

Turning to Britain, the compact tabby emperor made a big mistake in taking on the English sea-cat, Furatio Nelson: Napoleon should have observed that any cat with one eye and three legs, who was still standing, was going to be a tough one to beat. The cat population of Europe heaved a sigh of relief as Napoleon was exiled on St Helena. The deepest sigh came from his ex-chef, who bought himself a ten-year supply of frozen TV dinners.

*Napoleon Fishbone-apart in
typical understated lounge outfit*

COUNT DRACULA THE VAMPURR

*I*N THE SNOW-CAPPED mountains and winter forests of Transylvania, where there are more full moons than anywhere else, keeping warm is *very* important. Here, in Cattery Dracula, lives the inventor of fur-mal underwear: Count Dracula the Vampurr. He has been around since the terrible winter of 1539 and is only on the sixth of his nine lives, which he owes to keeping warm and getting to bed before dark. Joking about his rather prominent fangs he says: 'They come in extremely useful for opening tuna cans. Doesn't one just *hate* those ring-pulls?'

A martyr to his chilblains, the count was spurred on to his best creation: mountain goat-hair vests. The fluff is combed from the goats by very careful bats using their tiny, fine-gauge teeth. The goat and chamois wool is then woven into pashmina vests and long-johns, which sell extremely well to discerning cats worldwide. The count hopes to open another branch near Cape Town using fine springbok fluff – a suggestion made by his good friend, Vlad the Impala.

QUEEN VICTORIA AND PAW PRINTZ ALBERT

VICTORIA CAME TO the throne of England as a very young cat and ruled with a firm paw. She fell in love with, and married, Printz Albert of Saxe Coburg Gotha Holsten Pils Heineken, a noble Blue Prussian, and they had the biggest family in the Empire.

Albert soon adapted to British ways and shared his wife's love of the Highlands. He took to wearing a kilt in Scotland and kept a can-opener tucked into his sock-top, as the Scots do in case they run across a tin of wild red salmon.

Albert, a fervent sleeper, encouraged the Victorian spirit of progress by commissioning the finest brains of the era to find or build bigger and better beds for himself. When he finally went to the great feather bed in the sky, worn out by sleeping, Victoria was totally devastated. The colours 'Dark

Black' and 'Dingy Grey' were invented by crêpe and silk mills and the Queen wore one or the other or both for the next 40 years. She built endless memorials, statues, halls and embankments to his memory, named them all 'Albert' and had them inscribed 'REQUIES CAT IN PACES'.

The Albert Memorial

VINCENT VAN FLUFF

SOME ARTISTS HAVE painted with the mouth and others with the foot, but the Dutch painter Vincent Van Fluff decided to invent painting by ear. As Vincent is often depicted with a bandaged head, it is a popular misconception that he had cut off his left ear in a fit of rejected passion. This is nonsense; the truth is less dramatic: Vincent clearly needed to keep his best asset, when not in use, safely wrapped against dust, acid rain,

Seurat invents pointillism

overexposure to ultra violet rays, and so on. A daily mulch of sunflower oil kept the ear as supple as the best sable brush. Close examination of his masterpieces reveal that all the brush strokes are ear-shaped, and subjects like sunflowers were painted frequently because of their triangular ear-shaped petals.

Far from being pleased at the new movement that he had inspired, Vincent, ever one for strange moods, became restless and decided to move to Auvers and start painting views of cornfields. Looking around for an even more novel way of applying paint to canvas, he hit upon the idea of painting with a shotgun. This sort of thing can lead to unfortunate accidents.

Degas paints his ballet dancers by the nose

WHISKER WILDE

Some of the most frequently quoted witticisms and *bon mots* have flowed from the pen of this fine, eccentric wit and playwright. Whisker was large, languid and popular, and would have been nothing but successful if it were not for his one tragic flaw: he had a penchant for small birds. He developed a burning desire to run off with a golden-feathered canary, Alfred, who belonged to a pugnacious boxer dog called the Barquis of Queensbury.

Whisker eventually found himself locked up in Redwing Gaol for kidnapping the canary, but he was also known to have haunted the infamous catnip dens of Victorian London looking for young bullfinches and was once seen in Portsmouth trying to attract a wren.

Mrs Catbell in The Importance of Being in a Bird's Nest

RATSPUTIN

*T*HIS TALL, IMPOSING cat cast a long black shadow over a troubled Russia at the turn of the century. He wore the robes of an obscure holy order and possessed a devastatingly hypnotic stare. He was known in some quarters as 'the Mad Mink'.

At the time, Russia was ruled by the Czar, and Ratsputin soon came to have a powerful hold over the Royal Family because the Czar's wife hated rats with a passion, and the Winter Palace was teeming with them. No one seemed capable of reducing the rat population – except Ratsputin. He invented a clever device called 'cats' eyes' - the reflective glass dots which mark the middle of the road at night. He placed cats' eyes in a row along the road from St Petersburg town square to the river. Then he signposted this route 'To Oleg's – the best cheeseburgers in town'. In this way, coachloads of undesirable rodents were disposed of in no time. However, one day when Ratsputin was strolling on the frozen lake, rat frogmen, armed with a hacksaw, had their revenge.

PURRLOCK HOLMES

W HEN FOG AND crime were seething around gas-lit London in Hollywood-sized clouds, Purrlock and his faithful (but not dogged) companion, Dr Wotsit, were seeking the heinous Jack the Curtain Ripper. London hostesses were horrified to find their expensive curtains had been clawed to shreds during the night by the merciless Ripper, whose big mistake was to move into sofas. Knowing that once a serial shredder has tasted sofa there's no going back, Purrlock set a deadly trap: a sofa bed with a hair-trigger mechanism. This top-of-the-range Chesterfield, covered with William Morris jacquard and made up with Egyptian cotton sheets and 100 per cent lambs' wool blankets, was a temptation too far. The fact that it was the centrepiece of the Great Exhibition at the

Crystal Palace brought it up to mouth-watering status. The Ripper swung down from the glass roof and dropped lightly on to the bed. In a trice, the giant mousetrap mechanism snapped shut (as sofa beds will), neatly enclosing the captive Ripper.

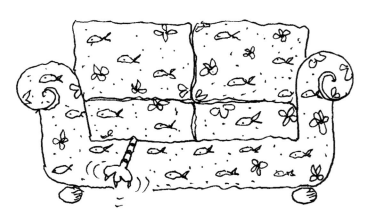

The demise of the Ripper

SIGMUND FLEA'D

*T*HE GREAT AUSTRIAN psychoanalyst was the first cat to interpret dreams as a way of getting rid of anxiety. Anxious cats came to him in droves. Miss X, lying on his famous couch, said: 'Herr Doktor, I had a terrible nightmare – I was telling my owner what I wanted for supper, how rare the steak should be and so on … and, horror! He did not seem to understand me!'

Sigmund Flea'd finds a creative way to overcome his envy of Jüng

'This is a common angst for many cats,' pronounced Flea'd, 'but it is irrational. Humans have been living cheek by whisker with cats for many centuries and are fully domesticated. Occasionally, there is the complete eejit who does not know how to use a can-opener. Those ones, sadly, we have to train patiently.'

One of Flea'd's pupils, Curly Jüng, also interpreted dreams. Flea'd was jealous because Jüng was jünger, curlier and Swiss. 'He knows nothing! He couldn't catch a cuckoo in a clock! The Swiss, huh. Their theories have more holes than their cheese.' Jüng, an expert on schizophrenia, muttered: 'I'm in two minds whether to tell him what I think of the Vienna ring road.'

Flea'd went on to invent the 'Flea'dian slip', a sort of anti-static petticoat that stopped cats' fur standing on end and crackling when clawing a nylon carpet, and the 'Super-Eggo', which is a mouseburger with cheese and a poached egg on top (later called an 'Egg McMuffin').

Jüng discovers that his cuckoo clock has a split personality

HISSADORA DUNCAN

*H*ISSADORA WAS FAMOUS at the turn of the century for creating freestyle dancing, usually with bare paws and in a cloud of chiffon scarves. Here, she is seen with her esoteric troupe in *The Dance of the Seven Voles*. This was a sell-out in London, Paris and Monaco. Unfortunately, four of the dancers defected to the Ballet Russe, and three voles couldn't quite cover the performance. The official censor stepped in and demanded future dances would be performed with double-knit woolly scarves but, somehow, the *frisson* just wasn't there. Hissadora's brilliant career came to an abrupt close when the tassels of her mohair scarf got caught in the propeller of a departing playboy's speedboat in Monte Carlo's marina – Hissadora shot over the horizon in four and a half seconds and hasn't been seen since.

Hissadora strolls in Monte Carlo

AL CATNIPONE
(THE GODFATHER)

1932, AND SMELLALOT NESS and the boys from the Federal Cupboard of Investigation were in Chicago. They were there for one reason – to find the Mafurrier boss, Al Catnipone, suspected brains behind the cod liver oil bootleggers.

He was not difficult to miss: he was standing on the corner of Furred and Main, blocking out the sun. He was not quite as big as a milk truck and he wore a suit so loud that his shirt had earplugs. His kipper tie could be seen

Dress your own gangster

*Scarface One-eye Mulloy was
not like other gangsters*

glowing from four blocks away and he had immaculate white sprats on his feet.

He greeted Ness with a friendly bullet. Fortunately, Ness was wearing his bullet-proof teeth. Although Ness's stomach was tougher than tanned vole hide, even he was sickened at the thought of what he had to do. He called in the one creature more dreaded than Catnipone himself – the Tax Inspector. Choking down a handful of bullets as tranquillisers, Catnipone turned himself in and begged to be locked up for his own safety.

SIR WINSTON CHINCHILLA

WINSTON WAS BORN a chubby and pugnacious kitten into the aristocratic family of the Dukes of Maulborough. A soldier and a politician, always keen for a good brawl, Winston also liked to argue and so he engaged in the Bore War – where MPs sat in the House of Purrliament to debate each other into a cata- tonic state. Later he took to broadcasting his speeches: 'We will fight them on the sofas …!' he growled, exhorting the listening cat population not to give up

Sir Winston Chinchilla gives his famous 'Victory' signal

prime sleeping quarters to despotic owners: '… we will fight them on the sheets! (on the blankets, on the cushions, on the hearth rugs, on folded angora jumpers, cashmere cardigans, toys …) we will never, never give in … we have nothing to offer but hisses, claws and teeth …!'

This popular policy (in place every since) ensured his position as Prime Minister. The cat owner's position has also remained the same: scrunched up on tiny portions of mattress with their knees under their nose, while the cat has 75 per cent of the bed.

Winston's ancestor, the Duke of Maulborough, mawling the enemy in a gentlemanly fashion

*H*ER FAMOUS CO-STAR, the laconic W.C. Fieldmouse, once described Mew as 'a full three pints of double cream poured into a half-gill measure' – and she certainly did ooze a wonderful, overflowing sex appeal.

She is credited with having invented the two-quaver purr and such throwaway lines as 'Is that a pilchard in ya pocket or are ya just pleased to see me?' Always playing the 'Spam Fatale' or slinky vamp, Mew became famous in Hollywood for her platinum blonde fur and her sexy walk. She could mince along the top of a neighbour's fence in a way that took your breath away; on a hot tin roof she was electrifying. Life for Mew was one long purr on a satin cushion.

Mew West in 'Cat on a Hot Tin Roof'

MARILYN CODROE

$\mathcal{T}$ HIS GORGEOUS, CUDDLY, white long-haired fluffball captured the heart of the film-going world. Her career specialised in public safety films, most famously *The Seven Year Itch*, warning cats of the dangers of letting fleas go uncontrolled; *Some Like It Hot*, advising against chilli-flavoured munchies as these can melt the whiskers; and *The Prints and the Show Cat*, with Pawrence Olivier. This film illustrated that even the most appealing kitten can endanger her pampered existence when pawprints appear on expensive bedspreads.

The curvaceous Codroe married other famous cats including Arfur Miller, a smart cat who could untangle balls of wool, get bells off cat collars and roll catnip cigarettes whilst boning a herring. Another husband, Joe di Magimix, invented the smoothly blended fish supper for elderly cats with slight dental defects.

MOUSEY TUNG

*M*OUSEY TUNG, AS his name suggests, was a cat of ineffable drabness. In fact, in the ancient oriental art of ditchwater impersonation, he had reached the tenth dan and could make Jane Eyre look like a gin palace floosie.

As a punishment for heinous crimes, Chinese prisoners were given the choice between having all their whiskers tweaked out or listening to one of chairman Mousey's speeches. There were a great many whiskerless ex-cons about at that time. Not content with having already bored the nation to a snoring standstill, Mousey decided that his daily mutterings were of such illumination that it would be a good idea to have them published, in his own *Little Red Book*, and allow the people the pleasure of learning them by heart. This proved to be an amazingly successful cure for insomnia.

To the vast relief of the nation, the end of Mousey Tung's regime came one day when, whilst visiting a camouflage netting factory near Shanghai, he blended in with the background and was never seen again.

RUDOLF FURRY-LEG

$\mathcal{T}$' HIS FINE, ATHLETIC, White Russian star of the Kirov Ballet was renowned for his astounding leaps: patio to top-of-fence, floor to wardrobe, stool to chandelier – no problem. He bounded over the Berlin Wall when he heard that Western Europe had taller wardrobes. There, he amazed audiences as he sailed over the highest fences, even in the tightest of tights. He teamed up with the exquisitely delicate ballerina, Dame Meeowgo Fonteyn, and could lift her to great heights. They leapt about together to such wonderful ballets as Pawkofiev's *Romeo and Juliet* and Tchaifluffski's *Sparrow Lake*. Sadly, Rudi had to retire after an unfortunate accident during a spectacular leap in *The Nutcracker*.

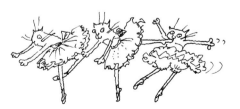

Corps de ballet

MOGGIE SCRATCHER

*I*N THE FIERY tradition of Bodice-Ear and Queen Elizapuss I, Moggie Scratcher (née Ratcatcher) has shown that the British can be governed by a female and a firm paw at the same time. 'The Iron Claw', as she was called, was returned to Parliament on a promise to bring down infleation – she frightened the living daylights out of the flea population who promptly quit the country.

Abroad, Mrs Scratcher would bash heads of state with her handbag to make them get into line for a photo. She was on equal terms with the then U.S. President, Ronald Ratgun,

The Scratchers at home

as well the ex-Russian leader, Mikhail Gerbilchops. However, she had her softer, maternal side: after a hard day's grey suit thrashing, she liked nothing better than to curl up on a cushion at No. 10 with her mate, Denis, and worry, idly, if their son, Mark, could find his way home in the dark.

ACKNOWLEDGEMENTS

The Cairo Museum (for the loan of Miaowpatra's fishing line).

The Asses' Milk Marketing Board.

The Swedish Herring Trust (founded by Erik the Viking).

Roman Villa, Catterick (for the mosaic of Clawdius).

R. Plantagenet (President), The Richard the Furred Is Innocent Society.

The Spam Foundation.

The Museum of Sardine Cans (Sam-mew-rai Armour Division), Osaka.

The Sioux Indian Appreciation Society, Dagenham.

The William Morris Bedding Co. (for Albert's four-poster and spring-loaded sofa beds).

Oleg's Cheeseburgers, Murmansk.

J. S. Bach. *The History of Music from Mouseart to Meatloaf.*

Colchester Museum (for fragments of Bodice-ear's Bronze Diners Club Card).

Catnip House at the Royal Botanic Gardens, Kew.

House of Commons Library, Westminster (for banned copies of *The Diary of A. Mole*, *Flycatcher* (Anon.) and Mata Furri's *The Spy Who*

Came in through the Catflap).

Julio's Taco-Shack, Mexico City (for the recipes for chocolate covered chilli-peppers *and* the antidote).

Tim Rice and Andrew Lloyd-Webber (for *not* setting this book to music).

The Earl of Southampton, *The Litter-Tray Works of William Shakespaw.*

The Royal Shakepaw Company, Scratchford-upon-Avon (for their inspiring performance of *Romiaow and Jellymeat*).

Lord Lucan, *The Mysterious Disappearance of Mousey-Tung.*

Won Fang (a 24-hour emergency dentist), Peking (for a plaster cast of Mousey Tung's molar).

L'Escoffthelot, *Regional Fish Recipes: Ajaccio to Archangel.*

Sir Arfur Conan Doyle, *Purrlock Holmes and the Mysterious Disappearance of Mousey Tung.*

Nick's Gallery, Athens (for a collection of Minnowan pottery).

Mewses Bagel Company.

Karl Manx, *Das Kapitail.*

Murray and McTavish Ltd, Aberdeen, who are the inventors and exporters of the 'Albert' combined can-opener, fish hook, fish hook disgorger, rat-flattener, mouse-mace, nit-flicker, tick-prong, claw trimmer, litter trowel and catflap spanner.

Jane's Chippie (Where you Seymour Seafood), Hampton Court.

The Hallam Stainless Steel Co., Sheffield (for Mrs Scratcher's spare claws).

Royal Maritime Museum, Greenwich (for C. Columpuss' curved telescope and Nelson's scratching post).

Mr Puddi Tatt (Manager), Ottoman Empire, Hemel Hempstead

Imperial War Museum (for the Duke of Wellington's recipe book).

Pawlo Printi (Curator), Temple of Pusseidon, Rome (for photographs of graffeeti attributed to Empurror Catigula [censored]).

Monsieur Purrcy of Salon de Sheen (for Bluey XIV's wig).

The wardrobe department at Metro Goldwyn Moggie Studios, California (for Mew West's combinations: saucy black-elastic collar/garter/catapult).